A BATTLE WITH THE DEVIL'S ENERGY

Published by Spines
ISBN: 979-8-89569-000-0

A BATTLE WITH THE DEVIL'S ENERGY

ALEXANDRIA FAIN

CHAPTER
ONE

I never thought a man could hurt me the way an ex-lover of mine did. But as I look at this growing experience as a huge lesson well learned, I never knew that I would go through and grow through the pain that I've experienced. But I have, and now I can truly say that I know the true meaning of "God gives His hardest battles to His strongest soldiers."

I said to myself, "Yes, God knew that I would succeed and get what He needed done on this earth through my true purpose." All of the things I didn't have the answer to started to come to me, one by one and piece by piece, as I continued on my journey.

As I was sitting on a chair outside, deep in my thoughts, visions flashed before my eyes of what had taken place and of what I had gone through, was going through, and what was to come. I was sitting there, deep in thought, as I started to think about a breakup I was going through. Don't get me wrong, I was so at peace, felt relaxed, and relieved with myself and everything, but as I thought about everything I've gone through and went through in my past relationships, it gave me the chills.

CHAPTER
TWO

When I say it was a whole mind, body, and soul-draining energy, it literally was—not just with my ex-man but with his family as well. When I say draining, I actually mean mentally, physically, spiritually, and emotionally. It was a battle, and not just a regular battle but a battle with the Devil and his attachments. I found myself all tied up and caught up in love and under a love spell with this man that I thought I could trust, not knowing that the whole time, this man was a shapeshifter as well as an energy vampire. I found myself quite a few times trying to leave this man, but something always pulled me back, literally, not knowing he was doing love spells on me, as well as stealing my energy, cheating, and using black magic.

Now, I remind you that I was deeply in love with this man from the beginning, and I knew nothing of black magic. Little did I know that the years 2020 through 2023 would be a huge eye-opener and awakening for me. When I say a huge enlightenment, I mean I was so shocked, amazed, and in awe. As I gained more and more knowledge of what was going on, I found myself left with no words to say and with my mouth open in amazement. I couldn't believe what this man had done to me. All of this time had gone by, and I was thinking he was one way when all the time he was wearing a mask.

It all started one summer night with a conversation we had over the Internet. During this time, I was going through a separation and breakup with my ex-boyfriend. Right during that time, my second child got sick with a bad cold. My mother took him to the hospital for me, and after they put him in a room and ran some tests, she then called to tell me to grab a few things because my child had pneumonia, and they were about to send us to Jackson, MS. As I was opening my bags and getting ready to head to the hospital, a message came through. If I had known it was the Devil, I never would have answered. Not knowing that this man needed to unmask and wasn't healed, I made a choice to answer the message, and when I did, I just couldn't resist talking to him.

CHAPTER

THREE

It was as if he knew all of the right words to say. He stayed making me smile, and we used to stay up all night on the phone as well. I knew the whole time that he was an energy vampire with an entity attachment. This had me hysterical, just sitting here thinking about all of this. I said to myself that this smoke wasn't enough and that I wanted to get some wine because this was just too good to be true. It could have been unbelievable, except it was happening to me, and this was so true.

Just thinking of this takes me back to when I asked Jay if I could move in with him, not knowing why I asked him to do this in the first place when I should have waited. It made me think back to when we first started meeting up. He would smoke a runt with me and drink some drinks with me, not knowing that he was trying to place me under illusions as well as trying to harm me.

Now, don't get me wrong. I always knew that I was psychic because of the visions I used to have when I was a little girl, but I have to say that I didn't see this coming. But as it came to pass and from that day forward, nothing was the same for me. My son and I had arrived in Jackson, MS, at the University Hospital for Children. We were getting situated when another message came in. I was kind of excited due to going through a breakup. I had gone through that breakup prior to meeting Jay.

As I was on mommy duty heavily at the hospital, I found myself texting back to back while my son and I were being taken care of. No lie, from the beginning, it felt so good to just have someone to say all the right things to you, to care, and to love you. It felt so wonderful until a couple of months had gone by.

Now, everybody has secrets and skeletons in their closet and things we've done in the past. But OMG, if I knew all the things that I know now back when we first met each other, I probably wouldn't have come as far with him as we had. Those were the same words I had just told him about a week prior to releasing him. We had come to an agreement that we were going to stay together and that I could move into his mother's house with him.

Of course, my children were spoken of from the beginning, and it was a known fact that I came with a package deal, meaning I have children that come with me as well. So, as I began to get settled in with Jay, everything looked good, but I began to see and notice the signs because he went from coming in on time to coming in way later and telling me the pettiest lies ever made up to tell. Every time he was caught in the act, I saw text messages out of the blue and would ask him straight out, "Who is this and why is she texting you?" Of course, then came his excuses, and this was only after a couple of months went by.

CHAPTER

FOUR

Yes, Jay told me that he was going to do right and that I didn't have to worry about messages and calls coming through out of nowhere from all kinds of women on different pages that he had. Of course, he was just lying to me, as it turned out, just to hold on to me, try to slow me down, and make himself look good while the whole time I'm here, and I'm a star. God is so good.

Yes, I ended up forgiving him, not knowing he had more mountains for me to climb already planned out. As I thought the messages would stop, they began to increase, and as they did, the phone calls did too—just calling and hanging up like some childish stuff. I then began to ask him if he was cheating on me, and yes, Jay denied it to the end.

So, I began paying attention to his routine, his ways, and the way he did things. I even began to notice that I had more feelings towards him than he had towards me. I started to feel like I loved him and had way more love for him than he did for me. I noticed that I gave him more attention and all of that, and now I see that it was due to me being placed under an illusion and under a love spell. This man had acted as if he cared so much when all the time he was out here doing the most behind my back while I was trying to give him the world.

I began to notice that he was very skilled at lying, manipulating, and putting stories together to make it seem like he was this or that, and to make it look as if everything was good when, behind the scenes, he was scheming and plotting the whole time. Come to find out, he was a people-pleaser as well.

CHAPTER

FIVE

I really treated that man like a king; I really did, when he was only a knight. I didn't understand and know that he was there to block my shine. But glory be to God, and I thank God so much for saving me from that situation. I did get to spend some wonderful holidays with him. He really liked my family, and he had seen how they loved me. He actually loved to be around them. I also began to find out that he was a shapeshifter, and this made me realize and acknowledge why certain things were being done.

I confronted this man and asked him so many times if he was cheating on me that it was a shame. I literally begged him for the truth, and he still lied to my face over and over again. For Valentine's Day, this man wanted to surprise me, and my cousin ended up helping him. I told him to wait, but he insisted. They told me to go to the truck and wait for a minute, and during that moment, I knew something was off. So, I got out of the truck, and as I walked to the door, I saw Jay jumping up and down behind my cousin. The first thing he said was that he was trying to keep me from coming in the door, and I automatically knew it, but they denied it. I let it go and told myself that I knew damn well this man wasn't messing with my cousin behind my back.

As we were living together at my mom's house, I began to notice an even bigger change. He began staying up all night and sleeping most of the day. All he wanted to do was play games on his phone, and he began to not even want to help me out around the house. Jay began to not pay me any attention, and, of course, being a woman, I started to speak up about this instead of letting it slide because he had already made me look bad enough. It seemed like the arguments didn't start heavily back to back until we moved into my mom's house. Jay started to act funny and strange and also went to sleep a lot. I asked him if he had gotten someone pregnant, but he said no. So, I looked over it and told him that if I found out someone was pregnant by him while he was in a relationship with me, he would forever be removed from my life.

As we were staying at my mom's house, I began to notice the difference even more. He began to leave six to seven days a week, then come back to me broke, busted, and knowing he had been out with his boys, clubbing, partying, hooking up with random females, lying, and slandering my name. Then he would want to come back to me and lie, saying he was trying to fix his car, knowing damn well he hadn't been working on any car. He knew he was lying to me in my face and doing me wrong behind my back while I was praying for him the whole time while he was trying to tear me down.

CHAPTER

SIX

During this breakup, I went through an enlightenment. I felt like no one had my back, even some of my family. As I was going through my rebirth, I thanked God, Jesus, the Holy Spirit, my angels, the archangels, my ancestors, and the ascended masters, as well as some of my family, for being with me during that time of my life because I had no one else.

During the time of my rebirth and enlightenment, I also began to watch tarot. I learned that, as well as watching tarot, I was actually being guided and that this was a part of my purpose as well. Yes, this was my destiny. Going through all of this during my breakup with my ex, and all the in-and-out he was doing and ghosting me, made me realize even more who I was. I began to release and disconnect from people, places, and things.

It hurt me so badly when that man walked out of my and my children's lives. I cried for days, wondering why he had abandoned me and left me out in the cold. As Jay was gone, I began to work on myself and give myself the self-love that I needed so badly. I also started looking up some dating sites, and that's how I met my false twin flame. Now, this was no accidental meeting at all. You see, just like my karmic soulmate, which means we have soul ties, my karmic was in lower vibrations, just like my false twin flame. I found out that they were all in lower vibrations as well after talking to him for almost a week. My soul knew the truth.

I told him exactly what was on my mind and what my soul felt and knew, and I left it as it was. Don't get me wrong, I called him maybe one more time and even sent him a text, telling him, "It's all love," because, as I said, my spirit knew the truth. After that, I never tried to call or text him again. I noticed how much he made me smile during the time we did talk, and as I look back, I smile even more, knowing why everything happened the way it did. I simply understood the assignment. So I then realized that yes, everything does happen for a reason.

CHAPTER
SEVEN

During that last breakup with my karmic Soul Mate, Jay, he asked if we could get back together, and we agreed upon doing so. But as we did, I also began to realize even more about some things that were going on, and I saw that I was around him and his family for a reason. Karma was calling for them and the things they had done and were doing behind the scenes. It was simply time for payback from The Most High. Of course, it is spoken that the year 2022 and beyond is the year of the Lovers and Balance.

I began to notice all the things that were starting to happen and that did happen to certain people that I knew and were close to me, but of course, not knowing who had spoken badly of me or about me and mine. See, that's where My Father GOD, JESUS, My ANGELS, Holy Spirit, My ANCESTORS, and The ASCENDED Masters come in. What I couldn't see, they could, and they go to war behind me. I thank GOD for them all.

So yes, as I began to watch everything and started to put everything together, I started to look at certain people differently. I also found myself not wanting to be around certain people, places, and things. I began releasing so much, including relationships, family, friends, foes, etc. In case you all are wondering, oh no, I'm not playing—I meant what I said. Releasing and cleansing is what I did.

I started to see from a higher standpoint that things about this family were off and not right or normal. You've got mothers who keep it real with their sons or daughters, telling them when they're wrong and advising them to leave someone alone before things blow up. But then you've got those mothers who keep it to themselves if they know their child is doing wrong, upholding the person in their wrongs. Of course, you can tell with the rest of the family too.

CHAPTER

EIGHT

Being the person I am—empathetic, a big Energy Reader, and a Psychic—I am a HIGH PRIESTESS as a whole. I would continuously overlook Lil's petty things and let them go when I should have been speaking up from the start. I began to notice how Jay's dad would talk to the mom so disrespectfully and foully that it was horrible. I saw why my supposed man began talking to me that way, as if I wasn't anything. But Jay had a choice to change, and he didn't want to. Jay had me all in my feelings, making me feel like I was doing something wrong or that I was the problem when the whole time it was him. I was uneducated about these types of games, and I didn't know Jay was trying to play this game on me. He must have really thought I was slow or naïve.

As the months went by, of course, we continued doing us. From the start, when we first got together, we weren't just going out to clubs, but Jay did have a thing for the club scene more than I did. I'm not a big club person, but I would step out to party every now and then, so it wasn't a problem. Then, boom—Jay started wanting to go out to the club more and more. With me being on mommy duty most of the time, I couldn't go without a babysitter. I noticed during the times we didn't go how it would affect him a little more than it did me. I would notice his attitude and all, but it wasn't quite sticking out to me like that.

Of course, me trying to hold it down and be the queen I am, showing him loyalty, not knowing all the time Jay was out to lie, steal, cheat, manipulate, and slander me. I noticed how Jay's mom always had her little ways of being sneaky and messy, lying to people and on people, and manipulating people as well. I noticed head-on how Jay's dad tried to start little arguments and throw shade like a big kid throwing rocks and hiding their hands, knowing all the time what he was doing. When you are too old for some things, you just need to sit down somewhere before GOD has the right match right in your face, and you wouldn't know until that karma hits. The backfire began to happen.

I sat back and watched even more and began to see and feel that the love wasn't real and that all Jay wanted to do was have sex.

CHAPTER
NINE

I'm going to keep it one hundred: yes, I like sex, but I can and have gone without it. When it came to him, it's like that's all he wanted me to do. After the fact, I asked myself how I didn't know he had a sex demon on him. How could I have not known about this? As I sat and thought on it, I remembered asking him numerous times why he was so sexually active, and he lied over and over. But I also see why now. I did not know that I was dealing with a narcissist.

We moved into a hotel and decided to stay there because we had not found an apartment, so we gave it a try. During our stay, it was like the fighting got worse. It was always something, mainly him not wanting to give me help. I already knew that he had cheated multiple times and wanted to constantly leave me hanging, with me mostly paying for everything and doing everything. This only made me want to end it, but why did I try to make it work? He began to throw me across the bed or on the floor. He would grab my throat and choke me, and depending on how far it went, he would hit me with his fists as well. But I am a woman, and fighting back is what I did because I was taught never to give up, even in the hardest times and situations. He only fought because he knew that's how I wouldn't leave. I didn't want to fight and didn't like to fight—at least not just for the sake of fighting.

I began to notice even more strange phone calls coming in, and I caught him sitting up many times. I would be sleeping and wake up to find him already awake, sitting beside me like he was watching TV. I asked myself a couple of times what he was doing while I was sleeping. I had the feeling that he had been sneaking out of the room and doing sneaky stuff while I was asleep. I was really fed up with everything that was going on. I tried and tried to make it work so many times, but I began to realize that the man I was sleeping with was in devil energy himself. I saw how materialistic he was, how stingy, and how cheap he acted when it came to things. The aggressive ways that started to stick out even more, and I noticed he only did things for a person when something was done for him or when he needed something done to the car.

As I observed the situation more and more, I began to lose the feelings I had for Jay. It hurt me so badly because he had love-bombed the hell out of me, and I didn't realize it until I had given up so much money, bought this and that, and spent so much time focusing on and trying to make things right for him. I wasn't giving myself the proper self-love, self-care, and self-nourishment I needed because I was too busy trying to take care of my children, myself, and a man who was barely helping me as he should have. When I say it hurt, boy, it did. I believe it hurt so much because I thought he loved me and my boys, but I found out he was all about what I had and what he could try to get from me.

CHAPTER
TEN

I began to show and give myself the self-love and attention that I had been giving him. I pulled back my energy and started to nurture and work on myself while he was out partying with anyone he could. I told myself that I had to move on because I knew he wasn't good for me. He was straight toxic, as well as some of his family members. I mean, they were straight karmic and lower vibrational.

You see, I didn't know much about energy vampires at first, but once I found out and learned what it meant, I could spot one a mile away. I was dealing with so much staying under that roof with that man and his family that it became unbearable. I knew I wasn't crazy, so I began to watch everyone in the house and those who came in and out. When I say watching, I mean observing their actions and how they moved. I even began to catch them in lies and arguments with one another. I overheard one telling the other, "You're laughing and talking to her right now, but you were talking about her behind her back." The other one yelled, "I didn't say anything," but I took all that in and heard it.

Do you hear me? I even had to sit outside in the car, in the freezing cold, just to smoke a blunt and calm down from everything that was going on and everything I was holding in and dealing with just to be with him because I thought he loved me. But little did I know, there was no love. I finally reached the point where I told him that I didn't need him and didn't want him, that I would be fine by myself, and I left him.

I began to experience blessings one after another as I acknowledged and asked Father GOD, my Angels, and my Ancestors for help and guidance. As I began to count on my Spirit Guides, I started receiving blessings. I began to reflect on a few instances when it seemed like he was trying to set me up. As I put everything together while deep in thought, it hit me so fast that he was trying to come up off a woman, and that woman just happened to be me.

CHAPTER
ELEVEN

I instantly began to cut off my emotions and feelings, realizing that it was just a cat-and-mouse game being played and I was the mouse. But what Jay and his family didn't know was who I was and who I am. You see, I am a Chosen One, a Starseed, and yes, I'm part of the 144,000. I'm also a Psychic High Priestess.

As I began to find out more and more about Jay and his family members, I also discovered more about myself and why they had chosen to mess with me in the wrong way. What I came to realize was that they thought I was young, ignorant, and wouldn't speak up about what they were doing to me. GOD already knew, but I guess they didn't believe that GOD cared or knew. They didn't realize that I was hidden in plain sight. Hell, I didn't even know it myself at first. There's no telling how many others had been mistreated the way I was, but little did they know that coming for this High Priestess Earth Angel would be their last mistake. Yes, they really messed up when they came up against GOD's Daughter, and that's what they didn't know.

I also started to find myself growing unattracted to Jay. Now, don't get me wrong—I was enjoying the head game; it was off the charts. But I saw that he always wanted it more. To me, it began to be a turn-off because it was like every time you looked, it was "I can't get any," or "Can I get some?" I was honestly getting annoyed because he didn't want to do a man's part by helping around the house or with the children. He just wanted to play the game and barely helped with the kids. Carrying all those extra burdens, I found myself tired, drained, and feeling like I wanted to forget it all—if not everything, then most of it. The lack of help was also draining.

CHAPTER
TWELVE

I was so sure that he was going to do right by me, but as more time went by, I began to see that he was really embodying devil energy himself. Don't get me wrong—yes, he played his part at first as a stepdad, but when I saw the mask slip, it was clear he was no longer fooling or getting one over on me. I woke up and realized that this man only wanted me for what I had at the time; other than that, there wasn't any love involved. By this point, I was all torn and cried out as well. I cried one last time because after the way he and his family embarrassed me, I promised myself that no matter how much he begged, I would get a restraining order so fast it would make his head spin. I meant it because the games were over, and I wasn't about to play them with him.

After the police ensured that I got everything that belonged to me, I headed out and was on my way back home. As I sat there crying to myself and regretting letting him back in, I began to pray and talk to GOD, my Angels, the Holy Spirit, and my Ancestors. While I was praying, I made sure to pour out my feelings, letting them know exactly how I felt, even though I knew they already understood. I then asked them all to help me and give me strength for my boys. After I let it out and talked to them, I felt as if a heavy weight had been lifted from me. I began to use my messages deck of cards, which confirmed and guided me as well. I already knew what my gut feeling had been telling me before, even before picking up the deck of cards. I knew he just could never admit or tell me himself, but of course, I knew. I even knew about the baby, and although I didn't want it to be true, it was, and I couldn't believe it.

As I sat there asking myself why, I immediately felt a chill go through my entire body and heard positive thoughts only. I knew that GOD, my Angels, and Ancestors were right there with me while I was shedding tears and talking to them. I couldn't believe that after all I had gone through with Jay, he would mess around on me again—not to mention the black magic he was doing, putting his hands on me, and slandering my name. But I bet he wasn't putting his hands on the ones he was out cheating on me with—well, at least I guessed not. Even though he hurt me, and it was eating me up inside that he was out there partying with another female or male, it hadn't even been one day—maybe not even a whole night.

THIRTEEN

I knew he had been out cheating on me behind my back and would constantly come running back to me like everything was sweet. There just wasn't any way in hell he thought that. I knew then that he really was tripping.

As I continued to think back before I packed my bags, I thought about what Jay's dad said when he called me a crackhead. I busted out laughing because that's all he could say, and I was like, "You could have really come better than that," because that man knew I didn't do crack. If you all could have seen the look on his face, it was priceless. The dad had enough nerve to beat me at calling the police when he was the one who started the whole conversation. I tried to call the police two different times, and Jay took my phone so that I couldn't call, but he let his dad ease back into their room, and he called. Little did they know, it wasn't going to go the way he thought it was.

What made me so mad with Jay is that he was supposed to have been my man, right? Like I said, but the dad called the police, and Jay made sure I didn't call. When the police came into the house, I politely told them what was going on. When I say this, you may not believe it. What he called the police for was so stupid that I couldn't believe it myself. It was because he told us that we needed to stop cooking because we had to burn out the stove. He said that we cooked about five times a week or so. The first thing I said was, "Man, what are you talking about?" because we had to eat, and I wasn't about to starve my children or myself. The conversation escalated from there.

I simply told Jay that he couldn't tell his dad right from wrong and that he didn't need to constantly be throwing shade at me and playing childish games to irritate me and get under my skin. What we had was over and done, not only because of that but also because they stood right there in front of the police, my face, and on camera, and all three of them lied and said that it had not been going on. I told the officers that this had been going on constantly and that the dad always had a problem with me. I also told them that all of them were energy vampires. I just really couldn't believe Jay took up for his parents when he knew they were wrong and lying. So to me, if you would get with them and lie about something simple like that, I knew he had to be lying to me about everything else. But it had me too hysterical.

CHAPTER
FOURTEEN

The only thing on my mind right then and there was that I better get the hell out of there quick, and that's what I did too. I just couldn't believe that I had been sleeping with the devil's energy all along. I would have never thought this just by looking at Jay and from being around him from time to time. I now realize that I had to be in his energy for him to do what he did to me, so I could go through what I had to grow through. I thought he had real love for me, but come to find out, he hated me and wanted what was mine. I found out that the hate was too real.

I began to think about two incidents, or shall I say situations, that had happened prior to this, and the first thing that hit my mind was "set up." That all of it had been a setup all along. I began to think back to times when his dad would come at me out of the blue, like I was somebody to play with because I was young. After sitting and crying, praying, and thinking, I knew why his family didn't like me. It was because my light aggravated their demons, and they thought they could energy harvest off of me. But it did not happen the way they thought, because I was out of there like white on rice and wasn't looking back.

It hurt so bad knowing that he had strung me along as if I was a puppet. He acted as if he didn't have a care in the world, the whole time knowing he had done me wrong. I recall asking him more than a few times if he was going through karma, and he would say "what" and shrug it off. But in my gut, when I first got that feeling, I knew, and my spirit knew the truth as well. I knew he cheated on me and had been lying to me about it faithfully every time, as if he wasn't. But I could sniff out that he was indeed a man Jezebel before my time. I tried to trust him anyway, not knowing.

CHAPTER

FIFTEEN

He was an energy vampire, and so was his family. When I say "straight narcissist," I mean a straight narcissist. For those of you reading this who don't know what a narcissist is, it's someone—whether a woman or a man—who is in lower vibrational energy, out for themselves. This person is mostly concerned with what revolves around them and them only.

The only reason I didn't know this from the beginning, when we first started talking, is because of the mask Jay and his family were wearing. When I say "wearing a mask," they were wearing it very well. But after a while, their masks began to slip off, and I began to see them for who they really were. He was with them every step of the way. So when I say they knew what was going on all the time and knew what Jay was doing to me, oh, believe me when I say they were with the games and stuff as well.

They knew the truth all along about what he was doing and what he had done. Come to find out, they were all together in it.

I went back to my mom's house to live there until I got an apartment or a house. I really didn't have a choice; I had to. Before I went back to Jay's house to stay, I was at my mom's house due to a prior breakup with Jay. That's why I say it was constantly going on with his parents being involved in childish games, and him too. I really dealt with a lot, and the thought of it made me shiver. I thought about the good times and bad times, seeing how he took me for granted all along. I began to think about how he used me and lied about all of it, and I felt a pain in my heart. It hurt a little more, and I felt my temples begin to tighten and ache. I closed my eyes, took a deep breath, and released to clear my mind, to release the pain my heart felt from what my false twin flame/lower-level soulmate had done.

CHAPTER

SIXTEEN

I continued to sit there with my candles lit, deep in thought, when it hit me like a ton of bricks why he was dealing with voodoo and black magic while trying to stop me from growing and being enlightened—toward it, on it, of it, or about it. I thank God every chance I get because, thanks to His love and help, He saved me. I'm very thankful and blessed for it.

It hadn't even been three days, and my mom and I had a few little words, which was something I didn't want at all, but it happened. It simply started because I told her that my hairbrush and my comb were missing. I said, "Mom, somebody must have been in this house," and she instantly started yelling, saying that I could go to my aunt's house because she didn't steal a comb or brush. I simply said, "Okay, Mom, but why are you yelling at me?" She just kept it going. I really wasn't up for any arguing, to be honest, especially not just after waking up to get my boys dressed for school—like, no way.

So, I called my grandma to tell her what was going on as my mom left out the door. You see, I'm not just a psychic; I'm an energy reader/messenger as well. I knew when I got up that her vibe was off, but I didn't say a word. The only time I did say something was to tell her my stuff was missing. I'll tell you what though—one thing I do know for sure is that the brush did not come up missing out of the blue; it didn't just get up and walk out of there. That's all I was saying.

I got back later that night, and my hair comb and hairbrush were still missing, so I didn't even worry about it anymore. My grandma had already told me before I left my aunt's house that day not to say anything else to her about it, and I simply said, "Okay." I noted to myself that since I had become single, the weather felt so good out.

CHAPTER
SEVENTEEN

I noticed that I felt so good, so free, so rejuvenated, and so intrigued by what was to come next. But at the same time, I was nervous and anxious, knowing in my soul that it was time for my new beginnings. I started to look back on what I had been through, but I shook my head and told myself to not look back and to just keep climbing higher and higher up those mountains until I reached the top. I was definitely about to pop and have my spot.

From that moment, I began to self-love and self-nurture my boys and myself even more, knowing that I was on Mommy's duty regardless of any heartache or pain. I began to focus on my boys and did what I had to do for us. It was my job as well. As I began to close that chapter of my life, I realized that I was about to start my new chapter as well. I was single as a pringle but didn't care too much to mingle. I was doing me and wasn't about to focus on the low vibrational energy from the chapter I was closing.

As I was closing that chapter, I also noticed that I had constantly been seeing angel number 1010, which means ending cycles and completion. I knew what time it was and started to see angel number 1111, which means new beginnings and new cycles. I was ready to begin these new cycles. Not all endings are bad, or shall I say the bad. Some endings/tower moments are for the good and to bring in the new and positive.

As I took all of my power back and gained control of myself, it felt so good to realize and know how free I was —mind, body, and soul. I felt, saw, and knew how hard my spirit guides, angels, and God were working for me. I knew they were helping me fight my battles, and I thank them for guiding and helping me through it all. From that moment, I knew how strong and powerful I was and who I was becoming.

As I began and started to set out on this new journey of mine, I began to think about what I needed to do the most for my boys. I started to shake off the old to let the new in. I began making plans and realized the lessons that I had just been taught and what I had recently discovered and learned. I laid my past to rest and closed that chapter in total.

EIGHTEEN

I started to lay out my plans and focus on what was mine: self-love and healing all in one. As I took my power back, I realized this man was trying to knock me down to my knees. I began to get everything together in my life. I was making major plans so that I could make major moves. The only thing I was missing was the money to make these major moves, because the plans and ideas I had in mind were sure to set the foundation for my empire. The only thing I needed was the money that I didn't have.

Now, don't get me wrong; I didn't need anyone because I knew exactly what I needed and how I wanted it to be. If I had the funds at that moment, I wouldn't have been seeking help from someone with the funds. So, I began to think about partnership. I didn't have a problem with partnership because I knew I needed help and that someone could use my help. I needed me and this person to be on the right page—mind, body, and soul. I began to pray to God for help.

I had just gotten back home from picking my children up from school with my cousin. We were chilling, and I began to have a vision of myself having dealings with my ex-boyfriend, not knowing he had only been in my life to create blockages. I thought about how he had tried to set me up and how he played a big role in trying to cause failure and burdens for me. I wondered why different problems had started to occur out of nowhere the way they did, and he was the diagnostic, which is known to be the problem of something, someone, or a certain situation. He was the problem all along, and I didn't think of this at all because I didn't know anything about the dark work he was involved in.

If I had known he was trying to stop my destiny, which he could never do, and if I had known that he was actually jealous of me, then I never would have been anywhere near or around that man, period. Memories flashed through my head of me falling asleep and waking up with no clothes the next morning quite a few times. I recalled asking him if he had touched me while I was asleep, and he would say no, he hadn't. I realized that I could really read Tarot and understand what it meant as well.

NINETEEN

I could understand Tarot as if it was meant exactly for me. I also began to gain my psychic abilities, reading energies and auras even more. I started to have epiphanies, then more visions and insight into certain people, situations, and things. I gained more and more enlightenment. I began to understand why my life had been so hard and why certain things had happened in my past relationships with the guys I had dealings with. I also started to see why I was put in certain situations and certain people's lives. It was because of who I am and what I was put here on this earth to do for my Father God.

Being me, I stood in my power and began to look at the mountain I had climbed up. I took a deep breath and began to congratulate myself on this great accomplishment I had just achieved. I was so happy, and it felt so good to be free and full of joy. I loved the skin I was in. I began to set out on my journey to fulfilling my destiny and my life purpose. I was ready to build this empire.

I found myself tired, stressed, and all worn down due to constantly giving Jay a chance. But I knew this time it was finally over, and his time was up with me. As the next day came, I began to regain my strength and started to lift myself back up.

TWENTY

I looked in the mirror and told myself, "You are beautiful. The past is over, and it is time for a new beginning." As I began to think about my Twin Flame, I started to use my intuition and psychic abilities even more. I began to meditate so that I could connect with my angels, spirit guides, and Father God regarding this situation, and I started receiving more messages and downloads about him as well.

I found out that he was married and wasn't willing to pursue this Life Purpose/Path. I discovered that he and his wife were working against me, even attempting to steal my identity. I also uncovered the lies and manipulation involving him. People were just being judgmental, engaged in petty "he says, she says" games. I let go of what no longer served me in dealing with those situations.

Jay was calling back to back nonstop, but I ignored all calls because I knew what he was after. He was draining me of my energy, time, and money. I realized this during the Dark Night of the Soul, one of the darkest times of my life. It felt like I didn't have anyone by my side. I was so stressed out due to what I had done while he was trying to affect my health, mental state, and physical body, and I discovered that the hard way.

I began to talk to God even more after realizing and understanding the favor He has on my life. I never knew I would have to go through what I had and was still going through, even with my mom. Throughout my journey, she was coming at me in the wrong way, as if I were the enemy, and had put me out two to three times due to our arguments. I told her exactly how I felt and stood up for myself like the woman I am. When I say my mom was treating me as if I were someone on the streets, that's exactly how I felt. And yes, it really hurt. But I prayed to God for help and a blessing so that I could get on my feet and move out.

The arguments were over little, childish things. I tried my best to ignore them until I could get out, knowing that this was my testimony. My own mother was acting as if she didn't care for me, with so much hate built up that it didn't make sense. I was ready to leave quickly. It was not right. I couldn't get over some of the scenes replaying in my mind; they were heart-dropping and unbearable. I just couldn't take it anymore.

I had been staying there for a few months when I started paying attention to my mom's behavior. I noticed how she would act towards me and the children at certain times. It was all an illusion.

CHAPTER

TWENTY-ONE

I thought back to when Jay moved into my mom's house with me, and I remember how she was acting so nice and accommodating. Then, all of a sudden, she changed her attitude and began speaking harshly to me over little things. I stopped caring, letting her talk while I ignored and blocked it out, especially when I knew she was trying to push my buttons.

I started observing my mom, as well as the rest of the family and Jay. I watched everyone closely. While I was still staying at my mom's house, I did what I had to do and stayed in my lane because I never wanted to get in her way. I really wouldn't have been there, but I had no choice. My aunt had said she didn't want anyone moving back into her house, which motivated me even more because I wanted my own place, car, and everything else. I knew I needed my own space for my boys and me.

I made a choice to be done with anything or anyone that didn't deserve my time, energy, or anything of mine. I decided to cut off everyone whom I knew and felt in my heart was not good or healthy for me and my children—family, friends, or foes. As I began to let go of people, places, and things that no longer served me, I started to feel much better, more relaxed, and relieved. It was as if I had so much built up, or shall I say pent up, that it hurt so much even as I was releasing it. But I began to release every tear that was within me, and the relief I felt was profound.

I immediately began to pray to God, asking for His help and for my angels to assist Him in helping me because I was hurting so badly and had no one to talk to. I asked God to help me with everything I was going through. Even though I had family, I had no one to talk to other than God, and that made me reflect deeply on everything happening around me. It struck me—damn, I really don't have anyone other than God, my angels, and my ancestors. I began shaking my head back and forth, focusing solely on my children, myself, and what was needed the most.

CHAPTER

TWENTY-TWO

I started to pray and talk to God more as I focused on my self-love and self-healing. I also began to grow more spiritually. As I reflected on everything, I knew the first thing I needed was a job as soon as possible, so I could begin working on my apartment and vehicle. If you asked me if it was hard to do so, I would honestly tell you yes, because it certainly wasn't easy, especially with little help.

I started looking for work to properly provide for my boys and myself. After a month and a half of constantly putting in applications, calling, and checking around, I finally got an interview. I was so happy because I needed to make my own money for my boys and me. But let's be real—I knew immediately that I would have to find a new job soon because the paychecks every two weeks barely covered my needs.

Don't get me wrong; yes, I was living with my mother and not paying bills, but I was in the process of trying to save money to move into my own place while ensuring we had personal items as well. I was barely making it off the paychecks I was earning, and I really needed higher payments. I was on the verge of walking away because I wasn't being paid enough for the work I was putting in. I was getting tired of it, but I knew I needed the money.

I started looking for a new job with higher pay. I was constantly working, managing my own business, and trying to get things the way I wanted and needed them to be. I was a single, young mother—often a popular loner and an up-and-coming star—working to get my life back on track after closing out a horrible chapter in my past.

TWENTY-THREE

I was so thankful and blessed as I continuously showed gratitude to GOD. I was at the house chilling and had just gotten out of the shower. I went to the store with my cousin and came back; we chilled and talked for a minute. My mother came out of the room, saying that I was too loud, and I told her that I wasn't that loud and that I was talking to my cousin.

I called my aunt and grandma to let them know what was going on. She said for me to leave her house because I was talking too loud and she wasn't going to get put out. Yes, I stood my ground toward her because it was as if she was constantly picking and doing things that were not right, as if I wasn't her own child. That was completely wrong to me. I was just telling her, in other words, that just because you're my mother doesn't mean you're going to run over me. I'm grown as well, and you have to give respect to get it. I don't disrespect my elders, so I knew that I shouldn't have been disrespected by an elder, especially my mother.

Some mothers will try to run over you, control you, put you down, or try to sabotage you because of the problems they have going on, insecurities, and lower vibrational ways that they will try to push onto people. Yes, some parents are like this. I had enough, and that was it for me. I was so tired of holding in everything and trying to be the bigger person when she was the mother and older person, but that didn't matter. I knew then that my mother was karmic and had lower vibrational ways and energy. Each time she has put me out, I sucked it up, gathering my boys and things, and left. My aunt talked to her, and she said that I could come back, but it wasn't the same at all. It became no love lost to me because I knew that a real mom wouldn't do anything like that. I was so fed up and done with it. It was sickening to me that my own mother was doing me the way she had done me. It was unbelievable, but I had the proof because it was happening to me.

I prayed, prayed, and prayed. I was focused and determined to bring myself up. I was a bottom girl survivor, and nothing was going to get in my way or stop me from reaching my dreams for my children and me. I was working my behind off to do what I needed, and I was praying to see more progress as well. I was constantly closing out chapters with family, friends, and others. I was cutting things off that weren't good for me left and right once I began to see clearly without a doubt in my mind, knowing that I was doing the right thing for myself, and yes, it was showing improvement as well. So I continued on my journey, closing out the old doors and stepping into the new doors that GOD was opening for me.

CHAPTER
TWENTY-FOUR

Yes, it was a change, but it was well worth it. I was elevating at an all-time high, and I must say that I was loving every bit of it and every minute as well. Yes, I was crying my eyes out at times, but it was well-needed emotionally, mentally, spiritually, and physically, and the release felt good afterward. I felt so rejuvenated, and I noticed, as I was walking into the new doors, that I began to see myself smile even more. You've got to know that, yes, I was loving it.

I started to move away from childish games, lies, illusions, and tricks, and I began to see my life improve so much more. I knew then that God was giving me the message that I was on the right road, on the right track, and passing tests. Once I knew this and learned of it, I started to gain more motivation to work even harder than I had been. I knew that I was out here swimming with the sharks, and since I was well aware of it, I paid attention to everything, especially anyone that was close to me.

I had grown and learned a lot since encountering the devil's energy itself and battling it among my ex-lover, his family members, and my family members, not including the people I didn't even know were hating on me for no reason. But it was all good because, as God says, they would always hate. But guess what? It's also said that every demon has to go to hell, so know that.

As I continued, I let go and let God. I started to be thankful for everything I had, everything I didn't have, and everything I would have. I continued to pray, keep faith, and believe that my prayers were about to be answered. I kept dreaming and manifesting with love.

www.ingramcontent.com/pod-product-compliance
Lightning Source LLC
Chambersburg PA
CBHW051333150726
47997CB00004B/1451